This book is about quotation marks. Do you ever use them in your writing? When?

Hi! My name is Steve Scoop, and I'm a reporter for the *Hoopletown Evening Herald*. My job is to talk to people and write down what they say. I have three important tools: my notebook, my pencil, and quotation marks.

I've just received a hot tip. Mr. McGillicutty is missing a pair of polka-dot socks. My boss wants me to write a story about it for the newspaper.

Quotation marks surround a person's words. That way, you know exactly what he or she said.

See, I've written down what my boss said in my notebook. I used quotation marks. Don't they look like they've captured the words? That's what quotation marks do. They're used to show the exact words that someone said.

Oops. My boss just told me to stop writing down every word she says.

I had better get to work. My first stop is the scene of the crime—Mr. McGillicutty's backyard.

Mr. McGillicutty tells me that, around 9:00 AM, he hung his wash on the clothesline to dry. But when he went out to get it at 11:30 AM, his favorite pair of polka-dot socks had disappeared!

When you quote people, you have the choice of putting their name at the beginning, middle, or end of the sentence. This time Steve chose the end, but he could also have chosen the beginning or middle:

• Mr. McGillicutty said, "My socks just disappeared!" (beginning)

• "My socks," said Mr. McGillicutty, "just disappeared!" (middle)

See, I've written down exactly what Mr. McGillicutty said. I placed his comments inside quotation marks. I wonder if his neighbors noticed anything suspicious. I better go investigate.

Now I'm talking to Ms. Slice. She's given me a really great tip.

Where did Steve place the speaker's name this time— at the beginning, middle, or end of the sentence?

I want to remember Ms. Slice's comment. So I wrote down exactly what she said. I've got to find out more about this mysterious Harold.

Here's Mike Montey, the mail carrier. He knows the suspect all right, and has some pretty alarming things to say about him.

Question marks go inside of the closing quotation marks.

This is incredible! Boy, I wrote down every word. This Harold sounds like a real bully.

Now I'm talking to a girl named Jenny Jennings. She's ten years old. Jenny says that, just a few minutes ago, she spotted Harold dashing toward the park.

Exclamation points are used in quotations when the speaker is talking either loudly or excitedly. Remember, exclamation points also go inside the closing quotation marks, the same as question marks.

Jenny gave me a really great lead. So I wrote it down. I'm hot on Harold's trail now!

What have we here? There's a pair of polka-dot socks lying on the ground. They are right beside a dog. Let's see if I can make out the name on his tag … Just as I suspected: Harold! Looks like I located the polka-dot sock thief!

To keep your writing lively, it's a good idea to find other words to use in place of *said*. For example, you could substitute:

- remarked
- laughed
- exclaimed
- reported
- commented
- whispered
- shouted
- sighed
- screamed
- barked

**Which one works best here? Can you think of some others? Brainstorm a list.**

Naturally, I wrote down Harold's statement. Looks like the case of Mr. McGillicutty's missing socks is officially closed. Now, I just have to write the story.

# ★Hoopletown★ EVENING HERALD

ALL THE QUOTES THAT ARE FIT TO PRINT 10¢

# MISSING SOCK MYSTERY SOLVED

## BY STEVE SCOOP

Harold

Mr. Clyde McGillicutty lost a pair of socks today. At approximately 9:00 AM he hung them on his clothesline to dry. Then, when he went out to get them at 11:30 AM, they had vanished. "My socks just disappeared!" exclaimed Mr. McGillicutty.

A neighbor, Ms. Enid Slice, suggested a likely sock-snatching suspect. "I'd bet my hat," she said, "that it was Harold."

Mr. Mike Montey, the mail carrier, agreed, saying that Harold often gives him trouble. "Can you believe Harold chased me down the street and helped himself to a bunch of letters?" asked Mr. Montey.

It was truly hard to believe. But this reporter was determined to find the footwear fiend. Jenny Jennings, age 10, provided a helpful clue. "I just saw Harold running toward the park!" she reported.

Upon arriving at the park, a pair of polka-dot socks was spotted lying on the ground. Nearby was a small dog. According to his tag, his name was Harold. Mystery solved. Asked what he had to say for himself, Harold replied, "Arf, arf."

In a late-breaking development, the socks have been returned to Mr. McGillicutty. He promptly put them on and is very happy.

Weather: Really Nice